...As Long As You Don't Turn Them Into Weirdos

Cousin Joanne —
I hope you enjoy our story ♡

Love,
Janell :)

...As Long As You Don't Turn Them Into Weirdos

Our Homeschool Journey @ The Smiley Academy

Janell Smiley

Xulon **Press**

Xulon Press
2301 Lucien Way #415
Maitland, FL 32751
407.339.4217
www.xulonpress.com

© 2017 by Janell Smiley

All rights reserved solely by the author. The author guarantees all contents are original and do not infringe upon the legal rights of any other person or work. No part of this book may be reproduced in any form without the permission of the author. The views expressed in this book are not necessarily those of the publisher.

Unless otherwise indicated, Scripture quotations taken from the Holy Bible, New International Version (NIV). Copyright © 1973, 1978, 1984, 2011 by Biblica, Inc.™. Used by permission. All rights reserved.

Printed in the United States of America.

ISBN-13: 9781545619681

To be perfectly clear, I am not a writer, nor am I a teacher. This will be no great literary work of art. I would simply love to share our story with you, and it is meant to be read as if we are sitting on the porch, drinking a cup of coffee or a glass of wine together, and you've just asked what on earth ever possessed me to do this. I hope our story encourages you and makes you laugh.

I wrote the following as a social media post the day our youngest son finished high school. The picture is not the best, but I love it. It was taken after shedding a few tears—both happy and sad—for coming to the end of our journey: entering attendance at the end of the day for the last time.

> He walks downstairs. "Mom, I turned in my last final . . . I'm done." And just like that, we are done. Bittersweet doesn't do it justice. This has been the biggest leap of faith I've ever taken, without question. It was also the best decision and most rewarding endeavor of my life. I feel incredibly blessed to have been able to do this with them and for them. It was not easy, but it was amazing. I wouldn't trade this experience and these years with my kids for anything. I am beyond thankful. If

...As Long As You Don't Turn Them Into Weirdos

I do say so myself, we knocked it way, way out of the park. As of this moment, I am officially retired from the position of head teacher and dean of boys at the Smiley Academy. It has been a joy.

I'll leave you with my husband's words to me after I told him my plan that fateful day nine years ago. He simply looked at me and said, "I'll support this as long as you don't turn them into weirdos." I think we did okay, and I'm thinking this will be the perfect title for my book.

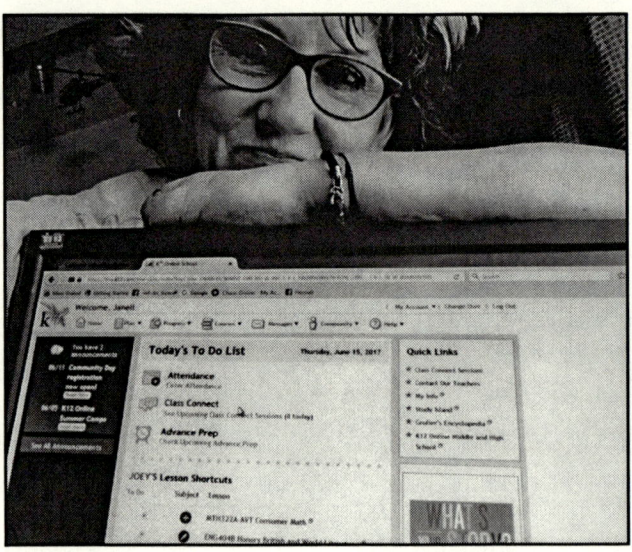

For Dennis, Jacob and Joseph
Love, Mom

In the Beginning

"I'll support you in this as long as you don't turn them into weirdos." Our journey started out with this being the most encouraging thing said. These were my husband's words to me after I told him I wanted to take our kids out of public school. I heard many less encouraging words. "Why on earth would you ever do that to yourself?" "What makes you think you could be successful?" "I can't wait for my kids to go away to school every day. I would never do that to myself!" "I can't imagine spending all summer with them after doing the whole school year at home!"

Yep, all of these words—and some even less encouraging—were said by family, friends, and strangers upon hearing that I was feeling led to try something different, something other than our neighborhood public school. Add my own doubts and fears on to that pile of negativity. What if I do turn them into weirdos? What if I really couldn't do this? After all, I was not a teacher. I had been an athlete, a band geek, and at best a moderately good student. Overall, I had been a fairly typical bored public-school student of the early eighties. I'd graduated from high school and matriculated to trade school after some classes at the local junior college. I'd worked hard, played hard, met my husband, fallen in love, gotten married, had kids, and sent them happily off to kindergarten. Nothing about my life experience indicated that I could be a successful homeschool parent—absolutely nothing.

Listening to His small, still voice is easier said than done. I began hearing it, feeling moved to do something after our oldest son's wonderful start in kindergarten. His first-grade year was when the voice became more insistent, more constant.

My kids are precocious; they're fairly bright, and they were ahead of the game from the start. They could read and do simple math before starting school. Kindergarten was great; it was a new and exciting time. Our teacher was a wonderful grandmotherly type of lady. We loved her, and I even sent her both boys' high school graduation announcements all those years later. We loved school. I volunteered in the classroom, and everything was great. To be honest, we liked all of our public-school teachers, and if I had to guess, my kids probably could have gone through the system and done okay. But I truly felt that we were supposed to do better than just okay.

In first grade, the kids were supposed to really get going on their reading skills. My oldest, Jacob, was more of a numbers guy. We read a lot at home and he was able to read on his own, but he'd rather do activities involving numbers, math, or building with blocks and Legos. He liked it when I read to him, and he would read out loud to me when I asked him to do so, but it wasn't his favorite. He had other things he'd rather be doing. So, this kid who was already able to do third-grade math was encouraged to join along with the class and do all of the reading, drawing, painting, and craft activities that made up the first-grade curriculum.

Very little math was happening in that classroom. Jacob began to complain about how boring school was. He started to say, "I don't want to stay there all day, Mom." I remember that first-grade parent-teacher conference. I was told by the sweet first-grade teacher that my high-achieving child had trouble reading and doing the fun activities like painting trees and houses. Hmmm . . .

"No," I said, "my son has no trouble reading. We read every day at home. He likes it. He reads to me all the time, but he'd rather do anything involving numbers, math, and building. He doesn't like painting pictures of houses and trees." (Irony alert: Jacob is in his third year of

In The Beginning

a master of architecture degree. There's lots of drawing pictures of houses and trees involved!)

I remember asking the teacher if there was any way he could do more math. Could we encourage the way this child was built? He was a math wizard, after all. Could we let him do math? She looked at me, and I could see that she was trying to be patient with this "difficult" parent whose "difficult" child pushed back against doing her version of first grade. She then said, "No, I can't facilitate that for him. He needs to do what the other children are doing."

The Downhill Slide

So, after that great start in kindergarten, the downhill slide began. Actually, if it had been a big, obvious downhill slide, I might have done something sooner. The change in our oldest was subtle at first but it gradually became a bigger deal to my husband and me because it started to affect his behavior at home. I ask you, should a first grader already be exhibiting signs of hating school? I don't remember hating it until junior high.

Jacob would come home from his day away at school in a truly foul mood. He would argue to the death about having to do his little homework packet. He would either sob or yell at me, "Mommy, this is so boring. Why do I have to do it?"

I didn't really have a good answer for him. "Because I said so and your teacher says so, that's why. It's how you'll learn."

He'd look at me like I was an idiot from another planet, and pitifully, angrily go about getting it done. However, he was 100-percent correct. It was boring, and at the tender young age of six, he had way better things to do. After tears and negotiations, he would settle down to do the little homework packet. He quickly learned that he could get it done through his frustrated tears in about twenty minutes on Monday afternoon and forget about it until Friday when he turned it in to the teacher.

By the end of first grade, Jacob was learning to hate school, and even worse, he was being taught to hate learning. To add another layer onto the pile of after-school fun we were currently experiencing, he began to cry every morning before school. Not only was this difficult, annoying, and exhausting, it was also heartbreaking! My sweet, smart child was turning into someone I didn't recognize. And I did nothing.

Your Kids Aren't Weird...

Well, not exactly nothing. I did start thinking something was wrong, either with my son, the teacher, or the school. Or maybe this was entirely my fault. That small, still voice became more insistent. As we went along through school and life, people were put in my path, particularly friends from church, who were doing school at home successfully. Their kids didn't seem too terribly weird. They were well mannered. They seemed very bright, and they were happy. We did a lot of life with these church people at the time. We were good friends, so I began to ask questions—many, *many* questions—about how and why they had decided to do school at home. Through their patient guidance and council, I began to research and ask more questions. I also specifically prayed about whether or not I should attempt to take on the daunting task of homeschooling. Hearing His small, still voice is one thing, but being bright enough to listen? That's a whole different ball game, and I was not bright enough or brave enough—not by a long shot.

I fretted and prayed for several years. I'm normally a confident, self-assured person, but for some reason, I just couldn't bring myself to pull the plug on public school. I mean, regular people just didn't do that, right? I had known a couple of homeschooled kids back in the day, and they were exceedingly strange. Why would a sane person embark on such a difficult and wholly consuming endeavor to have the end result be that your kids are too different and weird to do regular life? What if they couldn't find any kind of gainful employment or go to college? What if they didn't move out of our house? If I thought about it too much, I could easily seriously freak myself out. And I did just

Your Kids Aren't Weird . . .

that: I talked myself out of doing anything. And nothing changed.

Another year went by, and our younger boy, Joseph, started school and had an excellent kindergarten year as well. Jake and Joe are only seventeen months apart in age, which was two years apart in school. Joseph had the same sweet teacher his big brother had, and that fun, exciting year went by in a flash. Another good kindergarten student was headed off to first grade. After a more successful and much less boring second-grade year (which included learning lots of math from an excellent teacher), Jacob moved on to third grade.

And so it went for our family. We did regular life at regular school. In my oldest boy especially, the signs became more and more pronounced. Jacob became sullen, angry, and quiet. He needed an inordinate amount of alone time. I was told by the yard-duty teachers that he would not eat his lunch, and after a nice one-year reprieve (second grade), the crying came back. Every day after school, there was

...As Long As You Don't Turn Them Into Weirdos

some sort of epic meltdown. Every morning was the dragging of feet to get ready. "Mom, don't make me go to school! I hate it; it's so boring!" I was seriously considering taking Jake to see a shrink. And still, that constant buzzing was at the back of my brain. *You can do better. You should do something. Do something NOW!*

Finding Answers

It was the beginning of fifth and third grade for the Smiley boys. It was the beginning of October: time for parent-teacher conferences. I'd always been one of the moms who helped in the classroom and drove for field trips. I loved being able to see my kids in their school environment. They seemed well behaved and well adjusted, they had lots of friends, and they were not being bullied. In retrospect, I think I wanted to be there with them at school as much as possible without it being weird so I could find out why they both hated it so much. It just didn't make sense. Nothing pointed me to a clear reason for the way both Jake and Joe now acted away from school. According to them, school was the worst torture imaginable.

I went to that year's parent-teacher conference determined to get answers or, at the very least, an explanation for this disconnect. I liked Jacob's fifth-grade teacher, and so did he. Last year in fourth grade, my math-wizard child had started to do poorly on everything math related. He'd test through the roof in all the standardized testing, but he was bringing home math tests with big red Ds circled in big red ink and a big red "Please have a parent sign and return." He liked this fourth-grade teacher, and so he made just enough of an effort to get through without really complaining (or engaging) in any way. Because his standardized test scores were so high, the teacher let it all slide, saying she knew he was bright and it would be okay.

So, now I was here to make sure these bad habits and this negative trend were nipped in the bud. I crammed myself into the little desk opposite the fifth-grade teacher, a sweet lady. She said, "Jacob is a joy to have in my class,

Finding Answers

and isn't it fun that his classmates elected him their classroom president?"

"Yes, that's fun," I said. He hadn't told me this bit of "fun" information, and as I sat there, I began to wonder what else he'd been keeping from me. I remember asking the teacher if she saw anything at all that would have him hating being in the classroom. She was surprised; she couldn't imagine what I was talking about. As she'd just said, he was a joy and one of her best students.

"In fact," she told me, "he tested out of fifth-grade math for the start-of-year assessments. He had not one question wrong, even toward the end when they throw in a couple of sixth- and seventh-grade-level problems."

I asked, "Is there any way he could be challenged? He is extremely bored, and he cries every day before and after school. Could he please do sixth-grade math?"

She said almost exactly what the first-grade teacher had said: "I'm sorry; I just can't facilitate that for him."

Obviously, the next word out of my mouth was "WHY?"

She had several valid-sounding reasons: she had too many kids to keep control of, and there was too wide a range on the learning spectrum for her to take special time out for one kid who was already beyond proficient.

"Okay, then what does he do during math time?" I asked.

"Oh, it's wonderful. I use him as my math helper, like a teacher's aide!" she said enthusiastically.

It hit me like a ton of bricks. This was a big part of the problem. Jacob was bored and disconnected, and the bad habits were winning. School was becoming a place to barely try, to do just enough to slide through unnoticed. He hated being there, and now I could see why. This was *not* who he was made to be.

Little Brother Too

Helping to seal the deal for me was something that happened in Joseph's third-grade classroom. I was one of the volunteer moms, and at the beginning of the year, the kids did reading fluency testing, which I helped with. I was instructed by the teacher to set a timer to one minute and have the students read as fast as they could until the minute was up. After marking the stopping point, I was to count and record the number of words read in that minute.

I'm not entirely sure what this test was supposed to show; I don't think anyone knows. The teacher said it was just one of those hoops that had to be jumped through. One thing I learned from that silly test was that almost none of the kids could pass it. I remember very clearly that only four of the thirty-five kids I tested could pass at the level of proficiency set for third graders. That's a collective F. I came out of the little back room where the testing was done, and the teacher thanked me for my help and asked to see the score sheet. He shook his head and said, "Oh, wow, worse than last year; I'm not surprised. I'm not sure what can be done to improve these scores when half my class speaks English as a second language."

Joseph was one of the four who had passed. He had been claiming that school was boring for him as well. He hated to be there too, just like Jacob did. He would tell me that the teacher didn't control the class very well, and the kids didn't listen. He was having trouble concentrating and doing the work. He also said he felt ignored by the teacher. He'd been told that the other kids needed more attention and help since he was already doing well. Surprise! He started exhibiting all of the negative signs and behaviors of his big brother. He now fully joined in on the before-school crying and after-school freaking out. These two incidences—Jacob's parent-teacher conference and Joseph's reading fluency testing—were the proverbial last straw for me. I now knew I had to do something. I just didn't know what.

Stop Being Such a Big Baby!

At this point, I think it's important to note that my parents came straight out of the "If you don't stop crying, I'm going to give you something to cry about" school of thought. I continued my own slightly revised version of this parenting technique during these years, so if you think I babied my kids or tried to make excuses for them, you'd be wrong. I spent many years thinking I could teach my children that having a stiff upper lip, pulling themselves up by the bootstraps, and not being such a big baby would get them through their sadness and dislike of school to a place where everything would work out. My philosophy was that if you try really hard, you'll be happy and school won't make you sad. See how easy that is?

Needless to say, it didn't work. They did not become magically happy about going to school, and their father and I were exhausted from the emotional upheaval. It wasn't supposed to be like this. Smart kids are supposed to breeze through school and live happily ever after as successful adults, right? We didn't seem to be on track for this. In fact, at this point in the game, all I could see was years of struggle and strife, with my boys turning into depressed, angry underachievers who hated their parents for having ignored this glaring issue.

Miracle in the Checkout Line

All of this was weighing heavily on my heart. Still, I did nothing but double my efforts at fretting and worrying. Finally, after praying specifically for guidance and help, a week or so after our third- and fifth-grade parent-teacher conferences, I was standing in line at the grocery store. Waiting my turn, I was looking at the stuff on the checkout stand when a magazine cover caught my eye. In big, bold yellow letters, the cover said, "Are We Failing Our Geniuses? Why Smart Kids Are Dropping Out." I picked up the magazine and had just enough time to skim through the article.

...As Long As You Don't Turn Them Into Weirdos

I got goose bumps and felt completely floored. The article was about my kids, as if there had been a fly on our wall at home who'd flown back to the writer of the article and reported everything that had been going on for the past five years—everything I had been fretting and praying about. The story was about a group of folks who were frustrated with what was going on for their children in public school. Bright, high-achieving kids were becoming disgruntled and disinterested in learning. The author talked about some of the solutions these families had come up with, one being pulling the kids out of public school and starting a program with other families in the same boat. I put the magazine back in its spot on the checkout stand, paid for my groceries, and went home, knowing it was time to finally listen to the small, still voice that had just now become a shout.

Say Yes

When my husband came home from work that evening, I asked him to sit with me at the kitchen table. He did, then asked what was going on. "What's wrong?"

Poor man; he sat across from his wife, who was kind of freaking out. I felt almost crazed. I'm sure I looked the part! I was on fire with the decision I had come to while standing in the grocery store checkout line. It was time to make a big, scary move. I blithered at him in high-speed fast motion – literally all in one breath withnospacesbetweenmywords. I remember him sitting there with a fairly blank look on his face that most certainly did *not* match my excitement.

...As Long As You Don't Turn Them Into Weirdos

After a moment of awkward silence, I said, "Well, what do you think?"

He replied, "Ummm . . . well . . . I guess you're right; we should do something. I'll support you in this as long as you don't turn them into weirdos."

My husband, bless his heart, not only supported me, he trusted me. He trusted that I was trusting God, and because of that, he knew we'd be able to make this work. As I write this part of our story, I find I'm moved to tears—happy tears—remembering his reaction, his words.

Through the years, his role in this journey included being our tech support guy, solving any and all computer, scanner, and online lecture malfunctions. He was also my science helper. During elementary school years, he did several of the science lessons and helped set up the experiments, which included bending and scorching many a butter knife (I still have them), drawing on my Tupperware with permanent markers, and measuring, weighing, melting, and freezing all manner of items. Making a parachute for an

Say Yes

egg and tossing it out a second-story window for a physics lesson was a highlight. Luckily we had a whole carton of eggs; gravity was the clear winner for the first few attempts.

But mainly he simply left me to my task of doing everything else regarding the boys' education. The very best, most important thing my husband did was say one simple word: yes. Saying yes and trusting me, telling me, "You can do this," was his greatest gift.

Ripping Off the Band-Aid

That night, I asked Jacob and Joseph if they wanted to try doing school at home. "YES! YAY! PLEASE!" They had no idea what they were getting themselves into, but their enthusiasm was encouraging. I followed the advice of a friend who'd told me, "If you're going to take them out of public school, do it in one swift motion—like ripping off a Band-Aid." Talking about it and planning out a big, dramatic exit could backfire and make everyone anxious. It might also give me time to over think, worry, and second-guess myself. So, the next day during the drive to school, I told them that would be their last day of regular school. When I came to pick them up that afternoon, I'd tell their teachers. We'd go home and never have to come back.

In retrospect, I can see how that might have gone terribly wrong. That well-meant pep talk could have really freaked them out, making such huge changes in their little lives, but for some reason it didn't. Those two little boys got out of the car and went to their classrooms for the last time, and I went home to . . . panic. I spent the entire day thinking about what in the world I was going to say to the principal, the teachers, and the other parents. The way had finally been made crystal clear, yet I doubted. I fought my way not only through the doubt but the fear of the unknown. I got into the car and made that drive to school one last time. I was scared. What was I thinking!? I parked in the school parking lot and just sat there for a second, coming very close to chucking the whole idea. I took a deep breath, got out of the car, and walked straight to the principal's office.

I felt like I was in trouble, taking the walk of shame to the principal's office. I've only had to

Ripping Off The Band-aid

make that walk once. I was in seventh grade, and I had drawn a picture of my math teacher on my desk. She didn't like it (it was somewhat derogatory), and she turned me in. I had to go talk to the principal, and he gave me one afternoon of detention. This felt a lot like that. I had no idea what I was going to say and no clue what to expect from the person who'd been in charge of my children's education thus far. After being welcomed into her office and offered a chair, I sat down. She asked what she could do for me. I blurted out, "I'm going to take my boys out of public school. Today is their last day."

I expected anger or maybe even hurt feelings of some sort. I expected her to try and talk me out of this crazy notion, to offer a million reasons why this was a terrible idea. I expected anything and everything other than what the principal actually said: "I completely understand, and I think you will do a great job at home. I used to run a homeschooling program before I got this job. If you'd like, I can give you a name and number to call. This person will help get you started."

I'm pretty sure I sat there like an idiot with my mouth hanging open. That was the last thing I'd expected to hear. She did ask if I had any specific reason—had there been a problematic teacher in particular or anything at all that could have been done differently on the school's part. I gave her most of my reasons, telling her I didn't feel like the school was doing anything wrong per se, just that my kids were so bored and unfulfilled that they were becoming monsters at home. They hated school, and I needed to do something to change that. I'd tried everything else I could think of, and we couldn't afford private school, so here we were. The principal then stood up, shook my hand, and thanked me for meeting with her and for my honesty. She wished me good luck, and I walked out the door.

In a state of euphoric disbelief at how well that meeting had gone, I headed for Joseph's third-grade classroom. The bell dismissing school for the day had just rung. Kids came running out the door. I found mine and had him wait outside with a friend while I talked with his teacher. Once again, the unexpected happened. The teacher invited me in and shut the door when I said I needed to talk to him. I said, "This is our last day. I'm going to try doing school at home." He just stood there for a second. He got a little bit teary-eyed and said, "I totally understand, and if I didn't have to support my family with this job, I'd do the same thing for my own kids." He didn't even ask for a reason; he understood.

His reaction left me feeling somewhat sad, like I was breaking up with someone I really liked, but I knew had no future. I thanked him for the effort he'd put into my sons (he had been Jacob's third-grade teacher too) and for listening, then walked three doors down to Jacob's fifth-grade classroom. The teacher greeted me happily and asked if she could help me. I told her, and she started to cry actual tears. Now it was my turn to stand there in shock and get a little bit teary-eyed. She hugged me and told me she understood why I might make this decision. She said she'd miss my help in the classroom and my driving on field trips. She wished me luck, then hugged me and said goodbye.

The reaction from some of the parents was more of what I'd expected from the teachers: disbelief, anger, and lots of questions and concerns. Thinking they were out of earshot, someone mumbled something about how they felt removing kids from public school bordered on child abuse. There were also lots of hugs and well wishes. "I wish I was brave enough to do that too." "I'm going to take my kids out too." "Please keep in touch." "We will miss you." We made our way back to our car through all of this outpouring of sentiment and emotion. Both boys seemed excited and thankful. We were free!

Now What?

Oh, dear Lord, what had I done? In my most focused praying, I'd asked for my path to be made easy. If this was what we were supposed to do, I'd asked God to please make the path smooth. It couldn't have been made any smoother, but now what? My super-smooth path disappeared into a sea of doubt. I had the slip of paper the principal had given me, but for some reason, I felt frozen in place, unsure of how to start this endeavor. I had no idea what I was doing and no plan. Here, moments of real fear crept in. No, not fear; it was more like terror. I could very well and truly ruin my children. Perhaps we could show up to school the next morning . . . "Just kidding! Never mind, we're going to stay!"

NO. I pulled myself together and called the number on the little slip of paper the principal had given me, and once again, the path was made smooth. The person on the other end of the phone was very sweet and eager to meet us. She asked me a few questions and set up a time to meet in the next week. She also told me not to worry. "I know you might be feeling anxious and maybe even a little scared, but everything will be alright," she said. I remember asking what we should do in the meantime. She said, "Enjoy your kids. Go to the beach or a museum; do something fun together." She seemed to know something I didn't. She seemed confident that I was not going to ruin my children. Her message was, "Relax, decompress; you're going to be fine. I'll see you next week."

Easy for her to say. I imagined hearing a knock on the door and opening it to find several truant officers in dark suits and black ties wanting to question me and take my kids away from their unfit mother. Even so, we did manage to have a nice, quiet, no-meltdown couple of days. We did in fact go to the beach after sleeping in and celebrating our newfound freedom with a big chocolate chip pancake breakfast. The rest of that week went by, and I'm happy to tell you there were no incidences with truant officers. We had our meeting with the director of what was called the home study program.

Essentially, this was the public-school curriculum, no different from what the boys had been doing in regular school; you just did it at home. It had been set up originally for families whose children were dealing with an illness or injury that might keep them from being able to attend school.

Maybe I'm dim, or maybe it's just not put out there for the general public to know, but your kids do not have to do school in a classroom. Who knew? Not me, that's for sure. I mean, I knew people could do this, but I thought there would be a lot more to it. It couldn't be that simple, just making the decision to remove the children from school and start learning at home, could it? Yes, it was that simple! And guess what else? If college is a goal for your children, the way they do elementary school does not matter. Not one tiny bit. What matters is the development of their desire and ability to learn, and to *love* learning. *That* is what was being squashed in my boys.

First Steps

Our meeting with the homeschool lady went well. She had the boys read for her, and she asked them lots of questions. She asked me all kinds of questions about school and home, and she said something surprising. "You are not alone. For whatever the reasons, this is becoming more common. More families are making the decision to try something other than public school."

We left the meeting with arms full of textbooks, workbooks, and little kid novels. We set up a day to meet once a week with the nice homeschool lady, who was a retired public schoolteacher. She told me it might seem daunting at first, but to stick with it; we'd find our groove, and it would get easier as we went along. I felt encouraged, and the boys were excited. We were ready to get started!

My husband and I made a big deal out of turning the spare bedroom into a school room. Each boy got a desk, a roll-y chair just like Dad had in his office, binders, organizers, pens, pencils, a calculator, and, eventually, cheap older computers. We even bolted an old-fashioned pencil sharpener onto the top of a bookcase. We were ready—as ready as we could possibly be while having absolutely no clue what we were doing.

I didn't have a degree in education. I didn't have a teaching credential. I had become a CPR instructor in the mid-eighties, and I had also taught all grades of Sunday school for nine years or so. That was sort of like real teaching, right? Not even close. I'd never pretended to be a real teacher, believing it to be a true calling. It was something I had never been interested in or called to do. That being said, consider this: as parents, we are our children's first and most

First Steps

impactful teachers. When I looked at it that way, it helped me feel less anxious about potentially ruining my kids. After all, I was the one who'd taught them to walk, talk, and use the potty. As far as teaching went, I was batting a thousand!

So, we jumped in with both feet. We were officially homeschoolers! I was bound and determined not to turn our children into weirdos. I was going to prove all the naysayers wrong. We were not going to lie around in our pajamas all day without showering, like a never-ending sick day. In reality, that lasted about a month. In that first month while we were finding our way, I insisted upon a routine. We set the alarm, woke up, ate, showered, got dressed, and started school. It was more like a forced march than the fun, bonding, family-building, wonderful solution I had envisioned. I was so focused on not failing, not becoming that stereotypical weird homeschooling family, that I became overwhelmed and was missing the whole point. This was much more difficult than sending them off to school! Essentially, I became the one who

...As Long As You Don't Turn Them Into Weirdos

did the before-school crying and after-school melting down.

The kids, on the other hand, were noticeably calmer and more pleasant. Their personalities began to change, and our life at home began to smooth out considerably, with far fewer emotional upheavals and less drama than we had been experiencing previously. These changes were good, but I still felt unsure, and the actual doing-school part of our day seemed harder than it needed to be. Doubt crept in again until one day my husband came home from work and, after finishing cleaning up from dinner, said, "I've begun to notice that the boys are so much happier. The whole house feels happier and less stressed. And you are in a better mood at the end of the day."

He was right. They were . . . I was. Without realizing it, our entire family dynamic had started to change. The kids were their sweet selves again, and I was no longer playing the role of the Homework Nazi, which was our jokingly—albeit not really funny—made-up name

First Steps

for what I became every afternoon when the boys got home from school. My parents, who privately worried this was a bad idea but outwardly supported us and hoped for the best, even commented after we had spent a week visiting them. They told me there was a definite change in their grandsons' demeanor and behavior—a noticeable change for the better.

While all these good changes were happening, the main thing needing to change hadn't: the doing-school part of our day hadn't gotten any easier or better. The home study program had us using the same exact curriculum that had been so boring for Jake and Joe. Not yet willing to throw in the towel, we kept at it, meeting once a week with the nice home study teacher lady. During this meeting, we would turn in our work to be graded and receive the new week's work to be done. The boys were able to get their school work done in anywhere from two to four hours a day, so they had lots of time to do fun stuff like building with Legos and blocks, reading, and playing all sorts of games.

...As Long As You Don't Turn Them Into Weirdos

I backed off on the routine schedule enforcement and began to embrace that stereotypical homeschool weirdness. We slept in, and we *did* stay in our pajamas, sometimes all day. I was able to relax and enjoy my children again.

Let's Do Everything!

Following the advice of everyone on the planet in their well-meaning attempts to keep us from becoming too strange, I signed the boys up for everything. Okay, not quite everything, but close. Piano lessons, basketball, fencing, baseball, tae kwon do, Boy Scouts—you name it, we did it. We even tried a Dungeons & Dragons club, but this group didn't turn out to be our people. That was just fine; the D&D folks were happy, we just didn't like it, so we stopped going to the meetings.

I kept looking for things to do, ways to supplement our learning. We joined a homeschooled kids' ice skating group, which met once a week during regular school hours for hot chocolate,

...As Long As You Don't Turn Them Into Weirdos

war stories from seasoned homeschooler veterans, and ice skating. We had the rink all to ourselves, complete with instruction, games, and P.E. credit. We went to a local climbing wall with a similar deal for kids who do school at home. This was a great activity, and it was lots of good fun until Joseph, after some fear and trepidation, finally climbed all the way to the top only to freeze in sheer panic and terror. None of the adults present could coax him down. One of the climber dudes had to climb up and unstick the poor child's death grip. He was no match for terrified seven-year-old Joseph, who kept his hold on the wall no matter what the guy threw at him. The climber dude ended up just sort of peeling Joseph off the wall with extreme force, then letting him fall into his harness and dangle twenty feet up on the safety rope. We all had a good laugh and applauded the efforts of the climber dude. After wiping away his tears with hugs and comforting, my son announced that he was never stepping foot inside the climbing

Let's Do Everything!

center again. To this day, he has some minor trust issues with his mother.

So we found other things to do. We became members of the California Academy of Sciences, which entailed a quick trip into San Francisco. Spending the afternoon exploring this wonderful museum became a go-to activity for us as a family. If the day was going to be hot, we'd get school finished up quickly and go the beach. This was all great, but school was still the same old boring thing. I was beginning to wonder if there was a better way.

We'd met so many families who were doing school at home, and it seemed like all of them were doing something different. There are so many ways to learn these days, with unlimited resources, programs, groups, and gatherings. We had just discovered the tip of the tip of the iceberg, and I was starting to feel like it was time to make another change. There were so many choices. Everyone I talked with loved the way *they* were doing school: "You should try *our* program; it's the best!"

I felt stuck, unable to decide. We finished up our school year. Third and fifth grade were coming to an end. We had survived our first year of doing school at home, but I didn't know if we were going to stay on with the current program. I didn't have anything else in mind, with nothing new lined up for the next school year. That's when the next phase of our journey began to take shape.

A Better Way

I was in the front yard doing some pre-summer yard work when our next-door neighbor came out to her mailbox. I looked up from my weed whacker and said hello. She walked over to me and asked how we were doing—"How's the homeschooling going?" I told her it had been quite an adjustment, but it had been good. I said I'd been wondering if there might be a better program out there—a better way. "Oh, I have a friend who's a teacher with some sort of homeschooling program! I'm not sure what it's called, but I can give you her name and number if you'd like," she said.

I remember thinking, *What are the odds of that?* I felt like God had just plopped something good into our laps. Thankfully, there was plenty of plopping! Seemingly at every turn throughout the years, these plops happened at just the right time.

I called the number, and just like that, the next school year was all set up. We had a new and different way to do school in the fall. We had made it through that first year of doing school at home, but we were excited for summer, and I was also excited to try this newfound way to do school. It was called an online virtual school. I'd never heard of anything like this, but it was what was placed in our path, plopped in our laps. So, not knowing any better, we went with it.

Thankfully, it worked. It *really* worked. However, I'm not trying to tell anyone what to do; I'm not saying the way we ended up doing school is the best or only way to be successful. I know families who tried a virtual program and hated it. There are a million ways to do school outside of the public system. I've seen examples of all different types of curriculums and programs both work and fail. There's even something called "unschooling," which has no set curriculum or schedule of any sort, just learning by any means you see fit. I've seen it work wonderfully, with those kids going off to good schools and great jobs.

The moral of this part of the story is to find what works for your family and do that. If the first thing you try is horrible, then try something different. If doing school at home is a complete disaster for you and yours, then maybe public school is the right place. There is no penalty; just sign your kids back up.

Go for a Swim

We had a great summer, and another important piece of our puzzle fell into place. The Summer Olympics were happening that year, and we enjoyed watching as a family. Jacob and Joseph loved the swimming competition. They loved Michael Phelps and his total domination of the sport. This might not have been overly significant had the boys stayed in public school, but in my overzealous quest to keep them "socialized" and "normal" so the doubters wouldn't win, I thought something like joining a swim team might be a good fit for us. None of the other activities we'd tried had really stuck, and after watching a particularly exciting Olympic swim race, both boys said they wanted to learn to race just like the swimmers on the television.

Perfect! I googled swim teams in our town and found a big year-round competitive swim team. I e-mailed the coach and set up a time to have the boys try out. They showed the coach their swimming chops and were placed in the appropriate groups for their age and skill level. This is the one that stuck. They became competitive swimmers.

In retrospect, I see joining the swim team as another thing that was graciously plopped into our laps. Swimming became a solution to many of the things that could be seen as potential problems faced by removing kids from the classroom environment—you know, turning them into those strange, withdrawn, all-day-pajama-wearing weirdos. In a way, we found a huge extended family with three hundred siblings and all kinds of folks we spent a great deal of time with. We became close to some of these folks and remain friends to this day.

Go For A Swim

Swimming pretty much took over our lives for a good stretch of years. We had practice five to six days a week and swim meets most weekends all year long, with only a two-week break at the end of each summer. It was wonderful and horrible, fun and exhausting, but so completely worth it.

While my husband and I put in our mandatory volunteer hours, standing on the pool deck with all the other parents, stopwatch and clipboard in hand in the freezing rain, gale-force winds, and face-melting sun, our kids were having fun and getting massive amounts of exercise. They were gaining a skill and a hard-core work ethic, as well as the ability to push through pain, be it from swimming the mile or standing on the pool deck in a tiny Speedo at 5:30 a.m. in twenty-seven-degree weather, waiting for before-school swim practice to start. This was good character-building stuff. Spoiler alert: neither of the boys made it to the Olympics. Too bad, I know. Wouldn't that have made for a wonderful "yay homeschoolers" story? However, both Jake and Joe received many letters and e-mails from coaches of small-college swim schools, and even a few offers of athletic scholarship money from bigger schools.

As they got older, the boys turned their competitive swimming in the pool into some fun (but terrifying for Mom) open-water competitions. They did races to shore from Alcatraz, and also raced under the span of the Golden Gate Bridge. It turns out this was good stuff to put on college applications, being a fairly unique activity that helped them stand out to admissions teams.

In the Beginning, Part Two

Sorry, I got a little ahead of myself there. I was talking about that first summer. It was good, relaxing, and fun, and our newfound sport was in full swing. Fall was quickly approaching, and it was time to start our new school program. I asked the boys if they wanted to go back to regular school or try another year at home. They chose home. In fact, I asked this question at the start of every school year and even when they reached high school, a time when I figured they would want to go be with their people. However, they chose to stay home instead.

I'd done lots of research regarding online virtual schools and talked with people who either loved it or hated it. The folks who loved it did so because of the top-notch curriculum and its structure. The folks who hated it did so because it was too hard and too structured. We had the distinct advantage of having zero expectations and no idea at all of how this should go. We were a blank slate.

Toward the end of summer, the UPS man brought all kinds of goodies from our new school, including textbooks, workbooks, art supplies, and science experiment doodads. I got some cool stuff as well: teacher—or their term for those of us braving these waters, "learning coach"—workbooks filled with how-to advice and suggestions for planning and executing a smooth school day. A printer/scanner and computer rounded out the contents of the boxes sent from our virtual academy. Because "virtual academy" was part of the name of this new program, we dubbed ourselves The Smiley Academy as a fun joke and it stuck. We were the prestigious Smiley Academy, and of course our mascot was a smiley face.

The first day of school arrived, and we made a great big production out of it. The boys helped make a big special breakfast. We ate outside by

In The Beginning, Part Two

the pool just because we could. There was no hurry to get ready for school and out the door, no nervousness (although admittedly I was a little nervous), no tears, no "Please don't make me do this," "I hate school," or "Why do I have to go?" None of it. It was beautiful. Now it was time to get to work. We had taken the time before the first day of school to get acquainted with the new system. We'd looked through text books and online lessons, so there were no surprises that first day. The boys got to choose the subject they wanted to do first; they felt like they were in control. They liked it. I liked it. I quickly began to feel less anxious about ruining my kids' lives. This was going to work!

A new vocabulary made its way into our everyday lives. I was the "learning coach." We took "daily assessments," followed the "daily plan," ventured onto "Study Island," kept track of "weekly progress," went to "class connects," and logged in to the "online learning system," to name a few. We were assigned a homeroom teacher—a real, credentialed teacher who lived nearby. We met with her once a quarter to turn in work samples from each subject. She answered any questions I had, and the boys turned in writing samples, art samples, and science projects. She'd have each boy get the book he was currently reading and read out loud for her. It was her job to keep track of us and make sure I wasn't making a mess of things. I was definitely not alone in this venture, and there were standards to meet. This helped me feel more comfortable with my choice. We had a whole support system of folks to help us on our way and keep us on track. Our homeroom teacher was only a phone call or e-mail away, but unless I needed help, she left us to our task.

Am I?

At this point in the story I'd like to take a moment to address two of the biggest fears I encountered. Across the board, everyone I've ever chatted with about doing school at home had one or both of these concerns (me included).

1. I am not patient enough.
2. I am not smart enough.

With the last Smiley Academy student graduated and off to college this year, I can say that I was able to work it out despite all my shortcomings, and you will be able to as well. Let me tell you, I completely understand. Trust me when I say I almost let those two things stop me. First, I am generally a quick thinker, a snap decision maker, a fast talker, and it really bugs me when someone doesn't understand something I inherently understand. *How can you not understand this?* I think patience is a virtue . . . just not one of mine. Anyone who knows me well knows this truth.

Second, I did okay in school, not terrible, not great, just medium to medium well. Anything I enjoyed was an A. Anything I didn't care about was not an A. The thing I disliked most and cared about least was math. The thought of me being in charge of teaching math much past the difficultly level of sixth grade was frightening to say the least, a looming dark cloud in our otherwise happy homeschooling existence.

Let me explain. My father was an aeronautical engineer—quite literally a rocket scientist. This exceedingly nice man did his level best, bless his heart, to help me and my two younger siblings with our math homework throughout our scholastic careers. Our mom turned out to be the smart one: she stayed out of it. I don't remember much about what my brother and sister went through. Something tells me their experience was similar. My own math time at

Am I?

the kitchen table with Dad went something like this:

Dad: Okay, here's an example of how you do this. Now you try it.

Me: I don't understand.

Dad: Like this; it's quite simple, see?

Me: No, I don't see.

Dad: Here, try doing it like this.

Me: You mean like this?

Dad: NO. I don't understand how you can NOT understand this!

Me: I JUST DON'T! [Pitifully, feeling sorry for myself, with tears beginning here.]

Dad: LIKE THIS; TRY AGAIN!

Me: Like this? [Tears plopping on my paper.]

Dad: NO, THAT'S WRONG.

Me: DAD, THIS IS SO DUMB! Why do I need to learn this? I'll NEVER use it!

...As Long As You Don't Turn Them Into Weirdos

Dad: YOU USE MATH FOR EVERYTHING!

Me: I HOPE NOT!!!

At this point, my mom would peek her head around the corner and suggest that math time at the kitchen table with Dad be over before someone got hurt. As I write this part, I am truly laughing out loud at the memory; it is a good one. I wholeheartedly thank my dad for trying and my mom for being the referee. And guess what? I did use math for work later in life after all.

The scenario I just described is what was lurking in the back of my mind. Was I patient and/or bright enough to do a more successful, less ALL CAPS version of math time? I had to be. The bottom line was that this could be a deal breaker, a reason to quit, the reason the naysayers would win. Thankfully, oh so thankfully, my kids naturally understood math. They would've fared well at the kitchen table with my dad. Jake was starting sixth grade, and Joey fourth grade. I could've helped fairly well mathwise at these levels, but the boys were allowed to work ahead. Both were doing one grade-level higher, so for seventh-grade math, I was mostly useless as a "learning coach." I was more like the "learning water boy."

I Did It. So Can You.

Not *smart enough.* I certainly thought this might be the case at the Smiley Academy. Was I bright enough to pull this off? So, how did I win this particular battle with doubt? I learned that I could learn this stuff. I was able to teach myself, by the grace of God and the Khan Academy (an online site with step-by-step instructional videos for the math-challenged). Our new virtual program also did a good job trying to help those of us who had not majored in math at university, offering all sorts of refreshers and brushup help.

The boys' online lessons were succinct and to the point. If the boy understood the lesson, they could take the daily assessment. My rule was if they got 100 percent, they were allowed to move on to the next lesson. If there was trouble with a given concept and they didn't understand or get a perfect score on the little five-question daily assessment, there was a myriad of resources to help them learn. If that didn't work and they were still not understanding (thank God this did not happen often), and I didn't understand the concept either, I'd call for a timeout and go learn it for myself, then show the boys what I'd learned. They'd do several practice questions, retake the test, and score 100 percent. As the difficulty levels increased, I spent many an evening learning the math with letters and imaginary numbers after everyone else was in bed. Amid all this learning, I learned something surprising given my previous history with the subject: I liked math.

Not patient enough. I too feel this pain. I've heard, "I'm not patient enough," often coupled with, "My kids don't really listen me," from just about everyone who's ever chatted with me about the prospect of doing school at home.

I Did It. So Can You.

To be honest, if your kids don't really listen to you, doing school at home will be challenging to say the least. I'm a fairly large-and-in-charge sort of person. Keeping my kids under control wasn't something I struggled with very often. That being said, they most certainly tested my limits when it came to school time.

In our first year of school at home, we met once a week with the home study lady. That meeting served to keep the boys in check, if you will. Having to see her in person made them feel some accountability, and they had a desire to show her the good work they were doing. Changing to the online program in our second year of school at home meant no more weekly meetings. At first, I think Jake and Joe felt too much freedom. They felt like no one was paying attention to what they were supposed to be getting done on a given day.

My patience was tried and lost on a daily basis at first. We all had to learn to separate Regular Old Mom from School Mom. This was easier said than done, and I will fully admit to using the time-honored tactics of bribery and threats. Bribery came first. Monopoly money we called "school bucks" was used to encourage the boys to get all their work done with no argument or shenanigans. School bucks received for good work and good behavior could be redeemed to purchase treats and treasures. This worked well for the most part, but if bribery failed, all I had to do was threaten to put the offending child back into public school (most certainly in a raised—if not yelling—voice). I'm guessing this is an automatic disqualification from receiving the Parent of the Year award. That's okay; it worked like a charm.

The first year of virtual school was by far the most difficult. Technically, it was our second year of doing school at home, but this program was so different from home study that it was a complete reset for the Smiley Academy. We were back to square one, and we had to work out lots of kinks. My husband's computer nerdiness was a gift, because in the beginning, there were many technical difficulties. He was

I Did It. So Can You.

like a superhero who was able to fix everything always (eventually), and we were able to get all those kinks worked out. The sailing did eventually become smooth, and honestly, there's not a lot to write about here. We worked hard, got into our groove dialing in the whole online virtual school production, and moved up through the grades.

Less Me, More Them

Junior high was a little bit different. Instead of me being in charge of everything, the program introduced the concept of more of the daily assignments being done online rather than in workbooks. They were still doing the small daily assessment, while also adding bigger unit tests that were computer graded rather than Mom graded. The quarterly meetings were changed out for meeting with our homeroom teacher once a semester.

The junior high years went by fairly quickly and smoothly. Jake and Joe were becoming good competitive swimmers, practicing every day after school was done and attending meets most weekends. Both boys were invited to become members of the Junior National Honor Society in seventh grade. The doubt and fear I'd never completely let go of were fading into the background. Things were going well, save for an algebra hiccup or two. As we made our way through hyperbola, horizontal reflections, and common logarithms, I jokingly started saying as a way to lighten the mood when scary math threatened to darken it, "Math is your friend." This fun all-purpose phrase was meant as a joke, but it stuck with us through the years and even worked for college math.

But really, at the Smiley Academy, the subject that was most reviled was English—more specifically, grammar. The all caps "WHY DO I NEED TO LEARN THIS? I'LL NEVER USE IT AGAIN FOR THE REST OF MY LIFE" conversation happened for us with sentence diagramming. My wise and learned reply? "I have no idea why, and I agree: you'll never use it again. Now, stop arguing with me and get it done or I'll send you back to public school!"

Less Me, More Them

On to high school. At this point, my husband and I seriously considered enrolling our oldest in public school. We figured that if the boys were going to be turned into weirdos, this could potentially be when it happened: not going to high school with the other regular kids. We really only considered this for a brief moment. A simple listing out of the pros and cons, asking Jake if he wanted to try real high school (nope), and having some discussion about dedicating ourselves to seeing this through had us deciding to stay the course.

"But what about keeping your kids socialized?" said almost every single person on the planet. I find this question to be somewhat funny. The thought that the type of socializing going on at public high school is more desirable than some of the alternatives is, in my opinion, laughable. Please don't misunderstand. I'm not suggesting that public high school will turn your kids into drug-addled malcontent axe murderers. Not at all; in fact, the majority of our friends' children attended regular schools, and they are all lovely human beings who are doing life well.

What I *am* suggesting is that it's perhaps a bit narrow-minded to think attending public school is the only way children can become normal, functional, contributing-to-society types of adults. If you do school at home, you know (or if you are considering giving it a try, you will find out) that there are people out there—*lots* of people—who think (and will graciously share their opinion with you) that removing kids from the public-school classroom, finding other ways to get them out into the world, and learning and experiencing different things in unconventional ways with all manner of folks, is a bad thing. Essentially, they think you're ruining your children.

This is simply not true. In reality, one of the best things about it was being able to watch my kids quickly learn to become comfortable with all sorts of people of all ages, from old folks to babies, in any social situation. Did this happen because they didn't spend seven hours a day

Less Me, More Them

trapped in little rooms with forty other sixteen-year-olds? Truthfully, I don't know if there's any way to tell. Maybe someone should do an experiment. As always, just in case keeping them home was turning them into weirdos, we made sure to keep both boys busy in lots of activities to balance it all out.

Let's Dance

Joining the swim team was a very good thing, and both Jake and Joe swam competitively until the end of twelfth grade. As far as I'm concerned, among all the other activities done to keep them engaged in the community, two stood out above the rest. The first was another one of the things that was simply (thankfully) plopped into our laps: ballroom dancing at a local school of dance and etiquette that had been around since my own childhood. A couple of swim team friends, boys who'd either had older sisters or cousins who had participated in this wonderful activity, were going to sign up. Well, their moms were making them sign up. This definitely fell into the category of "Mom made us" for our kids. It's true; I did. Now that they're grown, both young men see ballroom dancing and etiquette as one the best things Mom forced them to take part in.

As you might imagine, there is always a shortage of male participants. News flash, guys: there are lots of girls there, and they will dance with you! A strict dress code was enforced. Boys, upon penalty of being sent home for the evening, had to wear a suit and tie, black socks, a belt, and dress shoes. Girls had to wear a modest, below-the-knee, no-plunging-neckline dress, low-heeled dress shoes, and old-fashioned fancy white gloves that kept the boys from sweating all over them.

From October to March on Tuesday nights, kids from all over our county got spiffed up and came to dance. Boys and girls were lined up and paired off, with the girls moving one space in line at the instructor's command so everyone danced with everyone. Parents didn't just drop off and leave; most stayed to watch. It was like a scene from a movie: beautiful, well-dressed young people twirling and dipping, being taught good, old-fashioned manners. There was no

Let's Dance

MTV grinding, drinking, or hickeys in the dark corner. (If you doubt me, chaperone a high school dance.) There was none of that, simply learning to waltz, swing dance, cha-cha, two-step, tango, all of it. This was ballroom dancing from days gone by.

After some initial whining about being forced to do something most boys think is dumb, Jake and Joe truly came to enjoy the school of dance and etiquette so much that they kept agreeing to sign on for the next session—four years' worth of sessions. The life lessons—how to comport oneself and dress properly for a formal setting, (say, a job interview) to be comfortable in fancy clothes, and to have good behavior—were priceless. Not to mention, the boys thought it was nice being one of those guys at weddings or college formals who knew how to dress and really dance. That was much more fun than feeling out of place and awkward. Attending the school of dance and etiquette has served both our boys well.

Giving Back

The second activity that kept our boys engaged in the community was gained through hard work: volunteering. Both Jake and Joe made the Dean's High Honors List all eight semesters of high school, and they were nominated by the teachers and counselors from our school program to be inducted into the National Honor Society. One of the requirements to maintain membership in the NHS was to complete a certain number of volunteer hours. Members were not to receive any kind of payment or accolade; they were just supposed to help out and give back.

It was more challenging than you'd think to find meaningful things for teenage kids to do. They needed to volunteer a minimum of six hours a month. At first, we did things like rake leaves for neighbors and pick up trash along our neighborhood creek trail. We'd given some time to the local food bank as part of a church group, but it turned out the food bank didn't want young teenagers on a regular basis. We tried the local animal shelter; they also had a rule that you had to be eighteen years old to volunteer. We didn't have the time constraints most other volunteers at work or school had; we could take an hour or two out of the middle of our school day, and because of this, we were able to find something that fit the bill perfectly.

The YWCA in our town runs a therapy preschool for at-risk kids aged three to five years old. These little ones had a rough start in life. They were either victims or witnesses of domestic violence in the home. Quite often, the violence was perpetrated by their dad or their mom's boyfriend—the significant male in the child's lives. The YWCA needed positive male role models who would be able to volunteer during the preschool's regular hours: during the school day. Jake and Joe fit the bill. They were interviewed and fingerprinted, then began spending two hours a week volunteering for the YWCA's "A Special Place" therapy preschool.

They helped do anything the staff needed: small maintenance tasks, yard work, and grunt work of all sorts. But mainly, they simply played with the kids. Reading, snack time, tag, pushing the swings, sandbox, you name it. Good, old-fashioned, care-free fun! My big kids were learning from these little kids the value of service, giving, and loving out of the goodness of their hearts for no compensation or reward other than the fact that the whole endeavor was a huge reward in and of itself. Volunteering with these sweet kids did more to grow and shape my young men than I can express. I simply can't do it justice. My husband and I are eternally grateful for this opportunity for both the impact it had on our boys and the impact they made on the preschoolers they worked with over the years.

I know for a fact this particular activity would not have been possible for us had we stayed in public school. It was one of the best things by far about doing school at home. The gold cord draped across the shoulders of first Jake and then Joe at graduation to signify membership in the NHS meant they maintained high grades, yes, but to me, it was more importantly about the time spent with those wonderful little kids at the therapy preschool.

This community interaction was gained through hard work, yes, but now that I think about it, this was also plopped in our laps. The way this opportunity came about was interesting. An old family friend I hadn't seen for many years had listed on a social media site that she was the volunteer coordinator for our local YWCA. I messaged her and asked what my then-younger teenage boys could do to help out, and it all fell into place. It was definitely a hard work–plopped combo.

Home of the Fighting Smiley Faces

During the high school years, my school roll diminished, as the boys had a real teacher for each subject and real councilors for high school, college, and their future careers. Going to class meant logging on to a "class connect" for the weekly lecture, which also included online debates and discussions. Everything was scanned and e-mailed to the various teachers for critique and grading. An excellent curriculum meant the boys stayed interested and engaged in the learning process. Because we didn't have the same time constraints and crazy homework schedule as regular school, the Smiley Academy students were able to take on as many Advanced Placement (AP) and Honors-level classes as they saw fit.

Math guy Jake was able to take every single math class offered, even taking two different math courses at the same time. He loved it! (This might verge on weirdo.) History buff Joe was able to take any and all history classes offered, also choosing to take more than one at a time. For Joe, one of these extra history classes was Introduction to Anthropology, which is generally not offered at public high school. The course description struck his fancy, and it turned out to be his favorite class. Anthropology and archeology also turned out to be his chosen college major.

If you're worrying about your kids being able to attend college after having done school at home, stop! Hindsight is twenty-twenty, and I admit that I did worry—a lot. When it became clear that both boys were going to pursue the goal of attending a four-year university straight out of high school, I began to have doubts and even nightmares where the kids got to their new college and were told on the first day of classes that they'd need to pack up and go back home—"Sorry, we can't allow you to attend because your schooling was inadequate." In those dreams, their lives were ruined and they hated me for the rest of my life. I'd wake up from this nightmare in a cold sweat and spend the day fretting once again about all the negative possibilities. It was awful. Had I made a huge mistake?

There's Nothing a Good Junior College Can't Do

I would be remiss if I didn't mention the fact that junior college can right all wrongs (should any occur) resulting from doing high school at home. It can also be the end goal, with your kids getting an associate's degree or training for a trade rather than attending a four-year university.

The public university system in our state has some very unique, unnecessary, outdated admissions requirements (as in, no other schools on the planet do things this way). Without going into a lot of detail, it all boils down in an oversimplified nutshell to this: if you do high school chemistry or biology at home instead of in a "real" classroom, don't bother applying to our schools. We didn't need to play this game, because from the beginning of high school, both boys had known they didn't want to apply within the public system. Several private schools in our state had sent recruiting letters, so they did apply to a few closer to home. And yes, private schools are expensive, but it's important to keep an open mind because *all* of them offer merit and/or need-based scholarship money if your student is accepted.

Knowing we didn't want to use our state public university system got us off that particular hook, so to speak, but the remedy to the previously mentioned admissions requirement is still simple: have your kids go to your local junior college. In fact, most of high school can be done at a junior college—usually at no cost to the student. So, just because we could, we gave it a try, with the boys taking a class here and there to see what it was like for fun, enrichment, and college credit.

Speaking of Enrichment

Another thing I'm 99.8 percent sure would not have happened had we stayed in public school was summer camp. No, not canoeing on the lake, arts and crafts, and food from the dining hall eaten at long picnic tables under the redwoods. Although the boys did attend a couple of those camps, I'm talking about career and college summer camp.

I'm pretty sure I wouldn't have bothered to research or inquire about something like this had I not continually been on the lookout for ways to deflect homeschooler weirdness. I also believe there'd be a fairly slim chance either kid would have willingly signed up for more sitting in a classroom after a whole school year of doing so. Maybe I'm wrong . . . maybe I'm not.

Suffice it to say that as we went along in high school and started to get ideas about potential career paths and interests, I remember thinking, *Wouldn't it be nice to know if what they're thinking would be a good fit?* Yes, it could—and did—save time and money for the boys to have a solid idea about what direction they might want to take.

When I Grow Up, I Want to Be...

From the age of two or three, Joseph loved airplanes and dinosaurs. He carried a little book about dinosaurs with him everywhere he went for several years. He even slept with it. I still have his bucket of a million little metal fighter jets. Finding a paleontology camp was challenging to say the least. They're out there, but they're very few and exceedingly expensive. Camps for fixing, flying, and designing airplanes were more plentiful and affordable, so the summer before tenth grade, Joey applied and was accepted to Embry-Riddle Aeronautical University's summer exploring aerospace engineering camp. It was an excellent program worth every single penny. He loved the campus, the other students, and the teachers—and he learned beyond a shadow of a doubt that this was *not* the right path for him.

At that summer camp, he learned he wasn't interested in the physics of flight, not to mention the fact that the thought of having to do that much math was abhorrent to him. Throughout the years, Joey's love of airplanes had begun to evolve into a love of history, starting at a very young age with the history of flight, the World Wars, fighter pilots and weapons, the people who used the planes, and the reasons they were at war. All of these books are still on his shelves. From there, his interest evolved into wanting to study ancient cultures and people, to dig in the dirt, and to learn all about how they lived and what had made them tick. The introduction to anthropology class he had taken in high school added fuel to the fire.

I remember him saying, "Now that I know for sure I don't want to study aerospace engineering, I know I want to travel and learn about people

When I Grow Up, I Want To Be . . .

all over the world." Armed with this knowledge, he was able to focus his college applications on schools with top-notch anthropology, archeology, and study abroad programs. He chose a school that also offered courses on paleontology. If you can combine all of that with your love of dinosaurs, why on earth wouldn't you? Also, I'll bet you five bucks Joey learns to fly in the not-so-distant future as well.

From the age of two or three, Jacob loved numbers and building things, from Legos and blocks formations to pillow forts and couch-cushion castles, which eventually evolved into drawing plans. He was always asking me to pick up another sketch pad from the grocery store. I've kept them all, stacks of drawing pads filled with floor plans for houses and buildings of all sorts. Not drawings of houses, mind you, with a door and a couple of windows, a tree in the yard, and a bright yellow sun in the upper corner of the paper. No, these were floor plans. To the untrained eye, they were just boxes—lots of different-sized boxes connected together forming the rooms of a house. He also drew maps, like the one on the inside cover of *The Lord of the Rings*. He'd make up a world in his head and draw out its floor plan.

In my mind (I think mostly because we have several engineers on both sides of the family) this all pointed to engineering of some sort. Jacob mostly agreed, so in the summer before tenth grade, I found and he applied to an exploring engineering camp at the University of Arizona. It was perfect; not only was it affordable, but it was near my parents, making for a nice summer visit after dropping Jake off at camp.

The program was wonderful, ending in a presentation in one of the big lecture halls. Each participant got up in front of the audience filled with friends and family and gave a PowerPoint presentation on a project they'd worked on. It was a proud moment for those of us there to support Jake. He did a great job, and when he was done presenting, he met us in the audience and said, "Well, the camp was fun, but I know I don't want to be an engineer." Okay, so

When I Grow Up, I Want To Be . . .

no engineering. Years of building and drawing boxes, floor plans, and maps could mean . . . architecture?

Yes, that's what it meant. All those clues topped off with Jake saying, "Mom, I'm supposed to be an architect. Not *want* to be. *Supposed* to be an architect." It turns out the kid knew what he was talking about. I found an inexpensive two-week exploring architecture program at the Illinois Institute of Technology. He applied in the summer before eleventh grade and was accepted. (As a side note, some of these programs were very selective, and getting in to one looks amazing on college apps. This was a nice plop in our laps without us realizing it at the time.) To make a long story short, Jake went to Chicago, attended this excellent camp, and returned home 100 percent sure that architecture would be his college major—and his life.

The ability to be specific on college applications resulted in several offers from universities—more specifically, from schools of architecture within said universities. "Know for sure what you want to major in? Come, let us teach you and give you lots of money!" This was a gigantic plop to be sure. The same went for Joey; applying specifically resulted in his being accepted into schools of anthropology and archeology. He was able to jump right in to his major with a "welcome to our family" from the dean and heads of those departments, complete with an invitation to travel to and participate in an active dig the summer before beginning his freshman year!

The College Pile

The nightmare scenario of my kids being banned from attending college, sent home because of the weird way they had done high school, never came to fruition. In fact, the opposite happened. I can't pinpoint why things worked out the way they did for us. I like to think it was simply a reward for taking that huge leap of faith. I've mentioned throughout this writing how things were sometimes plopped into our laps. All the "plopping" that happened throughout high school—and especially toward the end when it came time for graduation and college applications—was, I strongly feel, most definitely God sent.

Once all the hard work and dedication put into high school was coming to a close, with graduation coming up quickly, we sat back and accepted the plops as they fell, mainly in the form of recruitment, both academic and athletic, from all sorts of schools, both public and private, big and small, obscure and world renowned. Some included schools we'd never heard of, schools that were not on our radar, and schools that were much too expensive for us.

It took me a while, but I learned my lesson. Luckily, I'm smarter than I look, and this time I didn't hesitate to listen to the promptings: "Just have him apply." I knew we should just try even if we could never afford it, even if it seemed out of reach for him acceptance rate–wise. I began keeping the letters and e-mails, collecting the "college pile." The college pile remains on the schoolroom shelf to this day. I can't bring myself to toss it out. It represents the fruit of our labors, the end of our incredible journey, the result of finally listening and being brave enough to jump in with both feet.

The College Pile

During a gathering with friends, I mentioned the growing college pile. I was told by the folks who had college-aged kids that they received all those letters and e-mails too. It was all just advertising junk mail. Hmmm . . . oh well, I thought we were special. Silly me!

Luckily, I took the college pile off the shelf and really read through the "junk mail." I'm glad I did, because while a few of the pieces of mail were indeed advertising junk, most of it was not. I realized I was holding several Golden Tickets: invitations from admissions councilors and deans of universities saying things like, "We've noticed that your academics are a perfect fit for our school. Please apply; we are offering you a streamlined version of our application. We will waive your admissions essay, letters of recommendation requirements, and application fees. Just send us your transcripts and sign on the dotted line!"

Both boys took advantage of most of these special offers, but they also applied to schools that did not offer all this special stuff, so we did indeed go through the pains of writing essays and e-mailing/calling teachers to ask for glowing letters of recommendation. Both boys were accepted to a wide range of excellent schools, and both were offered big merit-based scholarships to the schools that wanted them.

Jake and Joe both were hoping to embark on an adventure—as it should be—after doing school at home in the same house and town they'd lived in all their lives. They were able to narrow down the offers and choose the schools that fit them best. My husband and I just returned home after a family vacation that included sending each boy off to school. We moved our youngest and last Smiley Academy student, Joseph, into his freshman dorm at the University of Wyoming, where he accepted their generous four-year scholarship offer and will major in anthropology and archeology. While getting Joey all tucked in, we sent Jacob back to New Orleans to start his third year of a master of architecture degree at Tulane University,

The College Pile

where he received a beyond generous five-year scholarship.

Just so you know, both of these schools fall into the category of *not* being on our college search radar, being way too expensive to bother applying (Tulane) and having never heard of them (there's a university in Wyoming?). Both schools sent a letter saying, "We want you. We love you. Apply for free," so I'm glad I took a second to look rather than tossing the college pile into the trash. Perhaps the biggest plop of all.

My husband and I are also incredibly thankful for these two vastly different yet equally wonderful places to visit. Our kids love their chosen majors, schools, and towns. Other than dealing with a new and fairly bad case of empty-nest syndrome, we couldn't be happier, more pleased, or prouder.

Are you wondering if I turned them into weirdos? The short answer is no, they are not weirdos. I mean, they were a little bit different to begin with. They are unusual without a doubt, being unique, sarcastic, funny, silly, quirky, confident, driven, hard-working, caring young men who didn't do school the way most kids do. If that makes them weird, then so be it. Things worked out wonderfully for this bunch of weirdos from the Smiley Academy.

I leaned on this verse in particular as I sent each boy off to college:

"For I know the plans I have for you," declares the Lord, "plans to prosper you and not to harm you, plans to give you a hope and a future" (Jeremiah 29:11 NIV).

I also leaned on this verse in particular throughout our journey:

"I can do all this through Him who gives me strength" (Philippians 4:13 NIV)

CPSIA information can be obtained
at www.ICGtesting.com
Printed in the USA
FSOW01n2142220118
43427FS